Stay At Home

A Collection of Poems

Nitya Baldava

NITYA BALDAVA

ISBN: 9798672360775

STAY AT HOME

DEDICATION

Dedicated to healthcare workers in line of battle against COVID 19 Pandemic and all children of my generation who stayed safe at home .

CONTENTS

NITYA BALDAVA

NITYA BALDAVA

THANK YOU

BOOKS
TEACHERS
FAMILY
HOME
WINS AND LOSSES

1. OUR LIFE

Our life is like a twisty road
Many acts disturb it just when it is doing
something
It carries a lot of load
It has to bear cars, and a person running.

Our life is like a wide-open flower
It would hate a big bad storm
It will be a sunshine lover
But hate a squiggly worm.

Our life is like a cloth
It can be sewn by a kind old tailor
Or be spoilt by a clothes moth
Its stitching, can also be a failure.

2. THE VIEW FROM MY WINDOW

I saw three hills in front of me,

Not so tall, but beautiful to see.

The first one full of grass and crops,

Just the spot where the goatsman stops.

The second one had some buildings on its side,

Obviously not a place where a car can ride.

The third one was the best,

With a grand castle on its west.

These are the three scenes I saw.

Now I'm off, to solve a jigsaw.

3. MY LOCKDOWN DAD

He sits lazily on the sofa or the bed,
He can't control his dozy head.

He sleeps and sleeps, day and night,
While playing he loses his sight.

He sees nine as six and six as nine,
I hope his eyes are still fine.

He eats all day,
Stop, stop! I say.

He is my naughty dad,
As fine as a young lad.

4. CLEAN MY ROOM

Oh! I have to clean my room
But listen, it's not with a broom

I have to keep it neat again
This thought keeps moving in my stuffed
brain

I have to pick up all the things
Papers, toys and game rings

I don't have space on the floor
So I tried walking on the wall and the door

The clothes are lying on the ground
I'd better start cleaning so I can move
around

Half of it done by my sister so small
But I'm the one who has to clear it all

I wish some fairies come at night
And make my room look fresh and bright

5. THE ROUTINE RIGHT NOW

Eat, sleep and play
That is my routine

At home, I will stay
And read a magazine

I will not study at all
That is my plan right now

I'll pretend not to hear when my father will call
When he'll scold, I'll ask when, what, how?

This is my schedule in the lockdown
So that the virus shouldn't strafe

I'll not go roaming in the town
So that I'll be safe

6. THEY TEASE ME

They tease me, they tease me, they tease me all day
They tease me from January to May!
They always call me different names
Especially when I get angry, losing many games.

I told them not to tease me in so many ways
We will, we will! my father says.
I cannot bear so many names at once,
They'll never stop as they've called me tons.

Being teased so much is a pain in the neck
Where do they get these names from, I'll have to check?
A nice scolding will serve them well
But I can't. You can obviously tell

The greatest teasers of all time, my good old dad
He always ends up making me very mad.
This is my poem, full of furiousness
Um, I guess I'll have to try to scold less.

7. SOUNDS AT HOME

The sense of being at home I love
Hear the rattling of utensils near the kitchen stove
Who would miss hearing the buzzing of fans up high?
Interrupted sometimes with a heavy sigh.

All the cheerful noise they make
Just a second it would take
In the morning, the birds' cheerful song
Then the bell goes ding ding-dong.

At noon the family chatting and chatting
And this is just the time to jump and sing
At night a lot of snoring all around
But we can just bear all that sound.

While in the hall you quietly roam
Hear all the sound, at your very own home

8. AN INTERESTING GAME OF CARDS

How to play an interesting game of cards,
For every type of human being?
Say Rummy or Uno,
For a game worth seeing.

For you hungry one,
When you play the ace of Heart,
Lick your tongue,
For a yummy cream tart

For you busy one,
When you play the ace of Diamonds,
Your work is done,
now count your funds.

For you silly one,
When you play the ace of Club,
To get some goody words in,
Your head you can rub.

For you funny one,
When you play the ace of Spades,
First you play,
Then laugh for decades!

9. WE CAN SAY

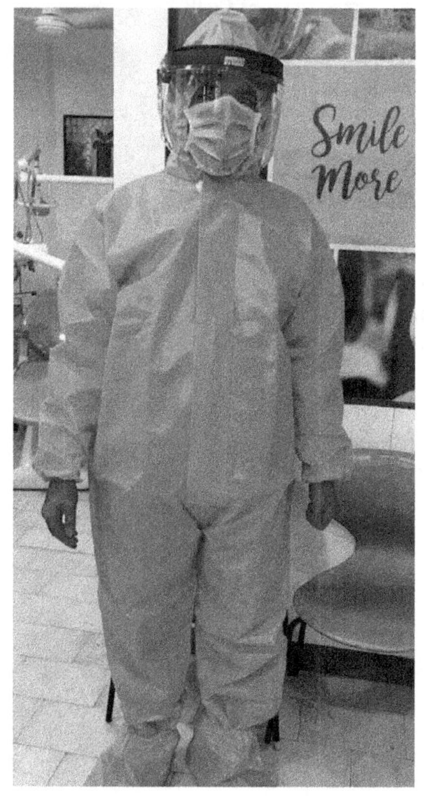

Thanks to the doctors, treating us everyday
A very hard job for them, we can say

Even when the hard days have arrived
Into the world of hard work, they have dived

How they work, with patience and kindness
We shall thank them, they never make a mess

Even the worst cases are cured by the doctors
In the current situation, they are the true saviors

Our gratitude towards them, we shall show
They are taking risks, all of us know

Happy doctor's day to all doctors
To all the true health issue warriors

10. TWO OLD RIBBONS

Two old ribbons
Shiny blue and orange ones

And on the sides of thee
Some thread we can see

Those ribbons good and old
in the same market they were sold

The two ribbons of no use
Somehow seem to amuse

Ribbons of unknown satisfaction
Go into my box, earning their own fraction

-Nitya
6/7/2020

STAY AT HOME

Two old ribbons
Shiny blue and orange ones

And on the sides of thee
Some thread we can see

Those ribbons good and old
In the same market they were sold

The two ribbons of no use
Somehow seem to amuse

Ribbons of unknown satisfaction
Go into my box, earning their own fraction

11. MY LITTLE..

STAY AT HOME

A cute little face full of glee
The happiest you would ever see

Shining marbles in her eyes
Not willing to say goodbyes

A nose, a sharp pointy one
The tippy edge, reflecting the sun

A mouth full of grandma's words
But sometimes as sweet as the song of birds

The curly hair, shining brown
Resembling the princess's crown

Hands holding the softest things
Deserving to wear the shiniest gold rings

Legs, posed with style and fashion
When troubled, a rocket run

Before I tell, who I'm talking about
Guess the answer, I'm not expecting a
doubt

She, my lil sisi whom I love so much
Beautiful to see, soft to touch

12. A GIFT FOR MY SISTER

I made a gift for my sister
Because she isn't a blister

That gift she loved so much
Who else can give a gift like such?

The gift was a house with a dog in it
In a basket, the creature would sit

'Woofket' the dog was named by me
It suited him, you can see

The cute little girl took complete care
She also fed it, while I would just stare

13. ALL THAT LOVE

That love I received everyday
How much? I can't say

For mine are the greatest parents till now
Their amount of love, they themselves don't
know

Grandparents who keep me safe and sound
They make me feel so good and bound

The best of all, my sweet sister
Nobody can be as cute as her

Aunts and uncles for some fun
For everything for me they've done

Cousins to fight and talk with me
My family is very big, you can see

My whole family, close to my heart so red
Grown bigger with all those adorable words
they've said

14. LOSING A GAME OF RUMMIKUB

You don't know how it feels
When you lose a game
They do not even cheer you up
Nor do they shout out your name

I wrote this poem so that they would understand
How it feels when you lose a game
When they would lose one
They would feel the same

Today I played a game of cards
But my father won
They didn't cheer me up
So, I would talk to none

ABOUT THE AUTHOR

Born in 2011, Nitya Baldava is a grade four student from Oakridge International School in Hyderabad, India. Verbal expression being her forte, she began rhyming in Hindi and English languages and created her own versions of popular kids rhymes in her early years. An avid reader, she draws inspiration from different genres and writers. Her writing originates from everyday events, observations, and at times from her own imagination. At the age of six, she chanced upon her father's journal of poetry and thoughts. Inspired, she began writing on her own.

www.ingramcontent.com/pod-product-compliance
Lightning Source LLC
Chambersburg PA
CBHW071240140726
47996CB00007B/2686